Jumpstarters for Properties of Matter

Short Daily Warm-ups for the Classroom

BY
ERIC T. OLSON

COPYRIGHT © 2009 Mark Twain Media, Inc.

ISBN 978-1-58037-488-0

Printing No. CD-404107

Mark Twain Media, Inc., Publishers
Distributed by Carson-Dellosa Publishing LLC

Visit us at www.carsondellosa.com

Table of Contents

Introduction to the Teacher

Students studying physical science have to keep track of many concepts and a lot of vocabulary. Getting them focused and ready for each day of class while helping them recall previously learned material can be quite a challenge. *Jumpstarters for Properties of Matter* is a great classroom companion for these purposes.

In the National Science Education Standards, the first key heading in the content standards for middle-level science is "Properties and changes of properties in matter." This book reinforces topics within this standard using a range of short warm-up and quick assessment activities.

The book begins by engaging students in describing and comparing general properties of objects like size, shape, and temperature. It then moves quickly to the idea that specific types of matter have characteristic properties, for example, density, melting point, or solubility. Later in the book, students focus on the notions of elements and compounds while exploring basic ideas concerning atoms and how they combine to form molecules of substances that can have properties different from their building blocks.

The most important way to keep track of atomic properties is the Periodic Table. Students at this level should not be expected to master abstract concepts about microscopic particles and atomic weights. Therefore, the activities herein on the Periodic Table focus on counting and repeating patterns (periods).

Suggestions for using warm-up activities:

- Copy and cut apart one page each week. Give students one warm-up activity each day at the beginning of class.

- Give each student a copy of the entire page to keep in their binders to complete as assigned.

- Make transparencies of individual warms-ups and complete activities as a group.

- Put copies of warm-ups in a learning center for students to complete on their own when they have a few extra minutes.

- Use warm-ups as homework assignments.

- Use warm-ups as questions in a review game.

- Keep some warm-ups on hand to use when the class has a few extra minutes before dismissal.

Properties of Matter Warm-ups: Forms of Matter

Name/Date _____

Forms of Matter 1

Write in the blanks just one word that describes what you might see, smell, or feel in each case.

1. _____ You rub your finger on the side of a glass.

2. _____ You see rain falling on the street.

3. _____ You pass the cosmetics counter at a retail store.

4. _____ You get out of an outdoor swimming pool on a breezy day.

Name/Date _____

Forms of Matter 2

Circle the correct word.

1. (Water / Air) is easier to run through.

2. Fires use (water / air) when burning.

3. (Water / Air) is easier to hold in an open container.

4. (Water / Air) is easier to see.

Name/Date _____

Forms of Matter 3

Fill in the blanks.

a. states	b. liquid
c. gas	d. water
e. solid	

Liquid water, ice, and water vapor are all forms of the same substance, _____. These forms are called _____ of matter. Ice is the _____ state of water. When water is in _____ state, it flows easily. When water becomes like the air and mixes with it, it is a _____.

Name/Date _____

Forms of Matter 4

For each state, write two examples of a type of matter you often see in that state.

1. solid _____

2. liquid _____

3. gas _____

Name/Date _____

Forms of Matter 5

Draw a line from the matter in the left column to how you would describe it in the right column. Draw as many lines as necessary if the matter has more than one method of comparison.

two different rocks   smoothness

water and air   hardness

two different pieces of metal   shape

steam and natural gas   temperature

                                       flammability

Properties of Matter Warm-ups:
Forms of Matter (cont.)

Name/Date _____

Forms of Matter 6

For each of the colors below, give one example of a type of matter that has that color.

1. blue _____

2. green _____

3. white _____

4. brown _____

Name/Date _____

Forms of Matter 7

Unscramble the following properties used for comparing types of matter.

1. D O O R _____

2. R T U E X E T _____

3. Z I E S _____

4. E A T T S _____

5. C R O O L _____

Name/Date _____

Forms of Matter 8

Choose a fresh food (not packaged or processed) that you like. Below,
list two properties you would like it to have and two properties you would not like it to have.

Fresh food: _____

Properties I would like my food to have:

1. _____

2. _____

Properties I would not like my food to have:

1. _____

2. _____

Name/Date _____

Forms of Matter 9

List two types of matter that have the following uses.

clothing _____

food _____

fuel _____

building materials _____

Name/Date _____

Forms of Matter 10

Check each item that has an odor you would recognize.

_____ Cooking gas   _____ Sand

_____ Spoiled food   _____ Paint

_____ Sawdust   _____ Metal

Striped Paint

Properties of Matter Warm-ups: What Is a "Property"?

Name/Date _____

What Is a "Property"? 1

Circle the words in parentheses that make the sentences true.

1. When the (size / temperature) of a liquid sample reaches its

    (melting point / boiling point), the liquid rapidly changes to gas.

2. When the (size / temperature) of a liquid sample falls to its

    (freezing point / melting point), the liquid begins to change to solid.

3. When a substance changes from solid to liquid or from liquid to gas, this

    is called a change of (size / temperature / state) of the substance.

Name/Date _____

What Is a "Property"? 2

Locate an object within your reach. Think of six different words to describe it, and write these words in the blanks. (The first one is done for you.)

_____size_____   _____

_____   _____

_____   _____

Name/Date _____

What Is a "Property"? 3

Write six different properties of matter that are *only* properties of an individual sample of a substance. These properties all could vary from sample to sample of the same substance.

_____shape_____   _____

_____   _____

_____   _____

Name/Date _____

What Is a "Property"? 4

Explain the difference between a property that depends on a given sample of a substance and a characteristic property of the substance itself.

_____

_____

_____

Name/Date _____

What Is a "Property"? 5

Rank the temperatures of each example of matter in order from coldest (1) to warmest (4).

a. _____ water in a swimming pool

b. _____ ice in the freezer

c. _____ soda from the refrigerator

d. _____ water and pasta boiling in a pot on the stovetop

Properties of Matter Warm-ups: What Is a "Property"? (cont.)

Name/Date _____

What Is a "Property"? 6

What am I? _____

Clue one: I am hard, solid matter where I am usually seen.

Clue two: You can find me in almost any size practically anywhere on Earth, just lying around.

Clue three: I can melt at high temperature, but you rarely see me in liquid form unless you live near a volcano.

Name/Date _____

What Is a "Property"? 7

Write "M" for mixture or "P" for pure substance.

1. _____ Distilled water
2. _____ Salt water
3. _____ Salt
4. _____ Lemon-pepper seasoning
5. _____ 24-karat gold
6. _____ Sand

Lemon Pepper Seasoning

Name/Date _____

What Is a "Property"? 8

Fill in the blanks.

vary	characteristic
water	melting point

Unknown matter can be identified through its _____ properties. These properties do not _____ from sample to sample of the same kind of matter. For example, the _____ of water under normal conditions is a temperature of 0°C, independent of the size of the sample. If you observe an unknown substance melt at 0°C, then you have information that could help you identify the substance as _____.

Name/Date _____

What Is a "Property"? 9

Fill in the blanks.

Sea water is a

solution	dissolved
mixture	water
matter	salt

_____

of many different kinds of _____. It is a kind of mixture called a _____ in which _____ and other substances are _____ in _____.

Name/Date _____

What Is a "Property"? 10

A pure substance might be an element or a compound. Explain the property that decides whether a pure substance is an element or compound.

_____

_____

PURE

Properties of Matter Warm-ups: Measuring Matter

Name/Date _____

Measuring Matter 1

Write a good definition of mass.

_____
_____
_____
_____

ANDY'S DANDY CANDY

500 Gr.

Name/Date _____

Measuring Matter 2

Write "Yes" or "No" to indicate if each statement is correct.

1. _____ A person's weight on the moon will be the same as on Earth.
2. _____ An object's mass stays the same if moved from Earth to the moon.
3. _____ Solids, liquids, and gases all have volume.
4. _____ A pound of cotton candy weighs more than a pound of rocks.

Name/Date _____

Measuring Matter 3

What am I? _____

Clue one: I am the International System of Units measurement unit for mass.

Clue two: On Earth, I am the equivalent of 2.2 pounds.

2.2 lbs = 1?

Clue three: There are 1,000 grams in me.

Name/Date _____

Measuring Matter 4

Change all the underlined words to make it a correct statement.

To measure the volume of a(n) <u>regularly</u> shaped object like a rock, place it in water in a graduated container. The <u>slope</u> of the water will <u>fall</u>, and that change in the volume of the <u>container</u> is the volume of the <u>water</u>.

Name/Date _____

Measuring Matter 5

Place the letter of the word next to the correct definition.

a. volume   **b. temperature**   **c. dimensions**   **d. weight**

1. _____ the average energy of motion of the particles in matter
2. _____ the lengths along each side of an object
3. _____ the amount of space that matter takes up
4. _____ a measure of the force of gravity upon an object

Properties of Matter Warm-ups: Measuring Matter (cont.)

Name/Date _____

Measuring Matter 6

Unscramble these SI units of measurement.

1. G A O R K I M L _____
2. M L E I L R I L T I _____
3. T E I E N C R E M T

   _____
4. R I L T E _____
5. B I U C C E R T E M

   _____
6. R A M G _____

Name/Date _____

Measuring Matter 7

Circle each true sentence.
1. Multiplying length, width, and height finds the volume of a rectangular object.
2. Solids and liquids have volume but gases do not.
3. There are no standardized units for measuring matter.
4. A milliliter is exactly 1 cubic centimeter.
5. Pressure is a force that pushes over the surface of an object.

Name/Date _____

Measuring Matter 8

A quick way to convert from temperature in Fahrenheit degrees to temperature in Celsius degrees is the "rule of 18." That is, a change of 18°F is the same as a change of 10°C. You know that ice melts at 32°F, which is 0°C. So, if you go up to 10°C, what's that in °F? The answer is 32 + 18 = 50°F. You would do the same going down, -10°C is 32 − 18 = 14°F. Use the rule of 18 to find these temperatures in degrees Fahrenheit.

1. 20°C = _____ °F
2. 30°C = _____ °F
3. 40°C = _____ °F

4. 5°C = _____ °F
5. -20°C = _____ °F
6. -40°C = _____ °F

Name/Date _____

Measuring Matter 9

Circle the correct words in parentheses.

1. A (balance / thermometer) is used to measure the (mass / volume) of objects.
2. The (metric system / standard system) is the standard unit of measurement in almost every country except the United States.

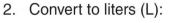

Name/Date _____

Measuring Matter 10

1. Convert to kilograms (kg):

   1,000 g = _____ kg

   10 g = _____ kg

   1,000 mL of water = _____ kg

2. Convert to liters (L):

   1,000 mL = _____ L

   10 mL = _____ L

   1 kg of water = _____ L

Properties of Matter Warm-ups: Density

Density 1

Write "T" for true or "F" for false.

1. _____ In order to find density, all you need to know is an object's mass and weight.

2. _____ Because a duck is denser than water, it must keep swimming to stay afloat.

3. _____ Mercury is denser than lead, so a lead ball would float in a pool of mercury.

4. _____ Using metric units, density can be expressed in g/cm^3.

Density 2

1. A softball weighs less than a basketball, but the softball is more than four times denser. Why?

   _____

2. A softball has a mass of 190 g and a volume of 480 cm^3. What is the approximate density of the softball in g/cm^3?

   _____

Density 3

In each pair below, one object sinks and the other floats. Circle the one you think would float when placed in water and explain why on your own paper.

1. can of regular soda   can of diet soda

2. kernel of popped popcorn
   kernel of unpopped popcorn

Density 4

Compare the behavior of a helium-filled balloon with that of an air-filled balloon.

1. Why does the helium balloon float in air?

   _____

2. The air-filled balloon sinks. Why?

   _____

Density 5

Fill in the blanks.

mass	property
float	volume
sink	

Density is a _____ of solids, liquids, and gases.

Two different objects might have the same _____,

but they can have a different _____. Since the

density of water is always one, objects with a density less than one

will _____, and objects with a density greater than

one will _____.

Properties of Matter Warm-ups: Density (cont.)

Name/Date _____

Density 6

The temperature at which water is most dense is 4°C.

1. Is water solid or liquid at that temperature? _____
2. Water is unusual because it becomes less dense as its temperature drops from 4°C toward the freezing point. Where will ice form on a pond, on the surface or below the surface?

_____

3. What is your reasoning in your answer to number 2? _____

_____

Name/Date _____

Density 7

Circle the correct words.

Both the (mass and density / weight and density) of an object are not affected by changes in gravity. An object will weigh less if brought from Earth to the moon, but its density will remain the same as long as it is brought there under the same conditions of (temperature and pressure / temperature and volume).

Name/Date _____

Density 8

What am I? _____

Clue one: I am transported across oceans in tankers.
Clue two: I am less dense than water.
Clue three: It's bad if I spill in the ocean, but if I do, my density aids in clean-up if I can quickly be contained.

Name/Date _____

Density 9

Write "Yes" or "No" for each statement.
1. _____ Objects of equal size always have equal density.
2. _____ Density is a characteristic property of an object.
3. _____ Two objects of different sizes cannot have the same mass.
4. _____ Small amounts of liquids more dense than water will float on water.

Name/Date _____

Density 10

Imagine you have a cold glass of root beer in front of you. Name two edible things that would float in the root beer.

1. _____

2. _____

Properties of Matter Warm-ups: Particle Ideas

Name/Date _____

Particle Ideas 1

Imagine that a "particle" can be any object. A "collection" of particles is a group of many such objects. On your own paper, give one example from everyday life of a collection of particles that more or less are identical and one example of a collection of particles that have distinct differences, but still form a "collection."

Name/Date _____

Particle Ideas 2

For each pair of objects, circle the one that would be easier to break into a collection of separate particles. On the blanks, explain why.

1. a piece of glass   a piece of metal

    _____

    _____

2. a bag of rice   a grain of rice

    _____

    _____

Name/Date _____

Particle Ideas 3

Rank the particles from 1 (the most) to 4 (the fewest) for the number of each you could fit into identical boxes.

a. _____ golf balls

b. _____ soda bottles

c. _____ sand

d. _____ televisions

Name/Date _____

Particle Ideas 4

Write "L" for the collections that are held together loosely and "T" for the collections held tightly together.

1. _____ Sand (on the beach)

2. _____ Particle board (used in building)

3. _____ Rice in a plastic bag

4. _____ Sand (used in concrete)

Name/Date _____

Particle Ideas 5

Fill in the blanks.

| mixture   Smoke |
| particles   colloid |

Sometimes large numbers of _____ are able to move

through air or water. _____ that floats through air is a product

that mixes with air when materials burn, releasing tiny particles. Milk is mostly

water and tiny, solid particles forming a _____ called a _____.

Properties of Matter Warm-ups: Particle Ideas (cont.)

Name/Date _____

Particle Ideas 6

Write "T" for true or "F" for false.

1. _____ Solids are made from particles with complete freedom of movement.
2. _____ Liquid particles stay close together when in a container, but separate easily.
3. _____ Gases aren't collections of individual particles.

Name/Date _____

Particle Ideas 7

In 1808, John Dalton proposed what model of the nature of matter? Describe this model.

_____

_____

_____

Name/Date _____

Particle Ideas 8

a. compound   b. atoms
c. molecule   d. elements

Fill in the blanks with the letters of the correct words.

1. A new substance formed from combinations of two or more _____ is called a _____.
2. When two or more _____ combine to form a new substance, the smallest particle of that substance is called a _____.

Name/Date _____

Particle Ideas 9

What does it mean when atoms bond?

_____

_____

_____

Name/Date _____

_____

Particle Ideas 10

Write the names of the three main particles that form atoms. Circle the particle that is involved in chemical bonding and underline the particles found in the nucleus.

1. _____

2. _____

3. _____

Properties of Matter Warm-ups: Properties of Solids

Name/Date _____

Properties of Solids 1

Write "T" for true or "F" for false.

1. _____ Plastic does not have a distinct melting point.
2. _____ You need heat to turn a solid into a liquid.
3. _____ If you dissolve a teaspoon of salt into a cup of water, you have turned the salt from a solid to a liquid.
4. _____ If you hold a solid long enough, you will be able to feel the particles that make up the solid move.

Name/Date _____

Properties of Solids 2

What are two differences in the properties of solids and liquids?

_____

_____

_____

Name/Date _____

Properties of Solids 3

Rewrite the passage on your own paper, correcting the underlined words.

Solids are made up of particles that are packed loosely together. They vibrate back and forth and remain in a random position. Because of this, a solid has a formless shape.

Name/Date _____

Properties of Solids 4

Solids have three main properties. What are they?

1. _____
2. _____
3. _____

Name/Date _____

Properties of Solids 5

Write "C" for crystalline solids or "A" for amorphous solids.

1. _____ sand
2. _____ glass
3. _____ rubber
4. _____ ice

Properties of Matter Warm-ups: Properties of Liquids

Name/Date _____

Properties of Liquids 1

Match.

a. viscosity	b. flow
c. fluid	d. liquid

1. _____ a substance that can flow
2. _____ the resistance of a liquid to flowing
3. _____ to move or run smoothly
4. _____ matter that takes the shape of its container

Name/Date _____

Properties of Liquids 2

Like solids, liquids are made up of particles. What is different about these particles that keep the liquid from holding a shape?

_____

_____

_____

Name/Date _____

Properties of Liquids 3

Write "T" for true or "F" for false.

1. _____ If you take 50 mL of water and pour it into a container that holds 100 mL, the volume of the water increases to fill the container.
2. _____ If you pour orange juice from a rectangular carton into a cylindrical glass, the orange juice takes the shape of the glass.
3. _____ Without a container, a liquid has no shape and will spread into a puddle.
4. _____ The cubic centimeter is an SI standard for measuring water.

Name/Date _____

Properties of Liquids 4

Circle the word in the parentheses that makes each sentence correct.

1. The (faster / slower) a liquid flows, the lower its viscosity.
2. You need to (heat / cool) a liquid to turn it into a solid.
3. The viscosity of a liquid is affected by (weight / temperature).
4. Liquids do not easily (compress / erupt).

Name/Date _____

Properties of Liquids 5

Imagine you have two sealed glass jars. One is half full of maple syrup and the other is half full of water. What do you think would happen if you flip both jars over at the same time? Why?

_____

_____

_____

Properties of Matter Warm-ups: Properties of Gases

Name/Date _____

Properties of Gases 1

What am I? _____

Clue one: I am made of tiny water molecules.

Clue two: My molecules move at high speeds in all directions.

Clue three: I fill all the space made available to me.

Name/Date _____

Properties of Gases 2

List three ways that gases differ from solids and liquids.

1. _____

2. _____

3. _____

Name/Date _____

Properties of Gases 3

Fill in the blanks with words from the list.

| compress |
| volume |
| container |
| pressure |

Gases are different from solids and liquids because they can change

_____ easily. Gas takes the shape

of the _____ it is in. Gas exerts

_____ on its surroundings and also is easy to

_____.

Name/Date _____

Properties of Gases 4

On a warm, sunny day, you decide to drive to the beach. Before leaving on your trip, you check the pressure in your car's tires and determine that it is within an acceptable range. When you return home that night, it's chilly outside. What do you think will happen if you recheck the pressure? Write your answer on your own paper.

Name/Date _____

Properties of Gases 5

Fill in the missing vowels in the names of these gases.

1. ___ X Y G ___ N

2. S T ___ ___ M

3. H ___ L ___ ___ M

4. N ___ T R ___ G ___ N

Properties of Matter Warm-ups: Physical and Chemical Changes

Name/Date _____

Physical and Chemical Changes 1

Circle the word in the parentheses that makes each sentence correct.

1. When a chemical change occurs, a (new / similar) substance forms.
2. A (precipitate / block) is a solid that forms from a solution during a chemical change.
3. Although a (physical / chemical) change can alter the appearance of a substance, it does not produce a new substance.
4. Energy is (always / sometimes) involved during physical and chemical changes.

Name/Date _____

Physical and Chemical Changes 2

Circle the correct words.

When (physical / chemical) changes happen, matter changes its shape, size, state, temperature, or other measure but does not change type. When (physical / chemical) changes happen, matter changes its shape, size, state, temperature, or other measure, and the matter itself changes type.

Name/Date _____

Physical and Chemical Changes 3

Imagine you are watching wood burn in a fireplace. List three things your senses detect as a chemical change occurs.

1. _____
2. _____
3. _____

Name/Date _____

Physical and Chemical Changes 4

Circle the item that describes a physical change.

1. crumpling a piece of paper
   burning a piece of paper
2. painting an iron gate
   allowing an iron gate to rust
3. molding clay   glazing clay in a kiln
4. digesting food   heating pasta sauce

Name/Date _____

Physical and Chemical Changes 5

Write "T" for true or "F" for false.

1. _____ All changes make different material.
2. _____ Ice changing to liquid water at room temperature is a physical change.
3. _____ Ice changing to liquid water using a stove is a chemical change.
4. _____ A color change often is a sign of a chemical change.

Properties of Matter Warm-ups: Physical and Chemical Changes (cont.)

Name/Date _____

Physical and Chemical Changes 6

List four different things that could be evidence of a chemical reaction.

1. _____

2. _____

3. _____

4. _____

Name/Date _____

Physical and Chemical Changes 7

Imagine you stir a spoonful of salt into a glass of water until the salt dissolves. Has the salt been permanently changed? Why or why not?

_____

_____

_____

Name/Date _____

Physical and Chemical Changes 8

Write "T" for true or "F" for false.

1. _____ Chemical reactions always produce gases.

2. _____ When two or more different substances combine chemically, the resulting substance can have different properties than the original substances.

3. _____ Physical changes never occur at the same time as chemical changes.

Name/Date _____

Physical and Chemical Changes 9

Fill in the blanks with words from the list.

| reactive   chemical bond   unreactive |

The force that holds together atoms of one or more substances is called a

_____.

_____ chemical bonds are unstable, while _____ chemical bonds are much more stable.

Name/Date _____

Physical and Chemical Changes 10

Read the paragraph to answer the questions that follow.

You decide to bake some cookies using ingredients you have at home, including flour, eggs, butter, vanilla, and baking powder. You mix the dough, bake the cookies, and allow them to cool.

1. Are any of these substances easily removed from the cookies after baking them? Explain.

_____

2. What evidence is there that at least one chemical reaction occurred during baking?

_____

Properties of Matter Warm-ups: Changes of State

Changes of State 1

Circle the words in parentheses that make the sentence true.

1. Below 0 degrees Celsius, water is in a (solid / liquid) state, and the water molecules are in (fixed / saturated) positions.
2. As ice melts, the water molecules (rearrange / stay fixed) and (do / do not) move faster.
3. Once water is at 100 degrees Celsius, adding more (energy / salt) causes water molecules to become a vapor.
4. As water vapor is heated, the water molecules move (slower / faster) and the temperature (rises / falls).

Changes of State 2

Write "T" for true or "F" for false.
1. _____ No two solids have the same melting point.
2. _____ Condensation is the opposite of vaporization.
3. _____ As matter is heated, the matter's molecules move faster.
4. _____ When you put liquid water into the freezer, the freezer's cold air causes the water to gain energy.

Changes of State 3

During the time a substance changes between solid and liquid state or between liquid and gaseous state, its temperature holds steady at the melting or boiling point. Why is this true? Write your best guess on your own paper.

Changes of State 4

Give an example of each of the two main types of vaporization.

1. _____

2. _____

Changes of State 5

Place a check next to the items below that are characteristic properties that could be used to identify a substance.

1. _____ Hardness
2. _____ Size
3. _____ Boiling point
4. _____ Melting point

Properties of Matter Warm-ups: Elements and Compounds

Name/Date _____

Elements and Compounds 1

Fill in the blanks.

solids	elements
liquids	particles
gases	

Substances exist that are made of only one kind of

_____.

These substances are called

_____. They exist

in nature as _____,

_____, or _____.

Name/Date _____

Elements and Compounds 2

Check the ones that are elements.

1. _____ Gold
2. _____ Carbon
3. _____ Brass
4. _____ Ice

Name/Date _____

Elements and Compounds 3

Draw a line to match the element to how it is used.

1. Iron   a. Animals need this for respiration.
2. Oxygen   b. Essential for fertile soil.
3. Chlorine   c. Required nutrient for building blood cells.
4. Nitrogen   d. Used to disinfect water.

Name/Date _____

Elements and Compounds 4

Pure substances can be formed from either elements or compounds. What is the main difference between elements and compounds?

_____

_____

_____

Name/Date _____

Elements and Compounds 5

What am I? _____

Clue one: I am a compound that plants need.

Clue two: I am found in the air in small amounts.

Clue three: Too much of me can cause the greenhouse effect.

Properties of Matter Warm-ups: Elements and Compounds (cont.)

Name/Date _____

Elements and Compounds 6

Write "T" for true or "F" for false.

1. _____ Some pairs of atoms have a strong attraction to each other and can bond chemically to form a new substance.

2. _____ In nature, metal atoms usually are found bonded to oxygen or other atoms.

3. _____ It's always easy to separate pure elements by breaking chemical bonds.

4. _____ Compounds are never formed from just one kind of atom.

Name/Date _____

Elements and Compounds 7

Write "C" for compound or "E" for element.

1. _____ Water
2. _____ Wood
3. _____ Hydrogen
4. _____ Silicon

Name/Date _____

Elements and Compounds 8

Place a check by the statements that are true.

1. _____ A new substance created by a chemical change is made of the same elements as the original substance.

2. _____ Elements may combine to make compounds.

3. _____ Compounds may be broken down into elements.

4. _____ Elements break down to compounds.

Name/Date _____

Elements and Compounds 9

Match.

| a. molecule |
| b. atom |
| c. element |
| d. compound |

1. _____ Smallest particle of a compound.

2. _____ Particle that forms an element.

3. _____ Substance that can't be broken down chemically into more basic particles.

4. _____ Substance formed from two or more types of atoms.

Name/Date _____

Elements and Compounds 10

Fill in the blanks.

| compound |
| properties |
| elements |

When wood is heated in a test tube, gas and liquid appear. This shows that a _____ can be broken down into other compounds or _____ with different _____ from the original material.

Properties of Matter Warm-ups: Where Elements Come From

Name/Date _____

Where Elements Come From 1

Is it easy to find elements in their pure form in nature? Why or why not?

_____

_____

_____

_____

_____

Name/Date _____

Where Elements Come From 2

Write "T" for true or "F" for false.

1. _____ Ores are minerals rich in metals.
2. _____ Oxygen bonds easily to many metals, so if you want to obtain pure metals, you often have to separate them from oxygen using chemical reactions.
3. _____ You never need energy to produce refined metals from ores.
4. _____ Gold does exist in nature in pure form.

Name/Date _____

Where Elements Come From 3

For the following examples of element separation, write "C" if the process is chemical, "E" if it is electrolytic (involving electricity), or "Ph" if it is physical.

1. _____ Iron is obtained in a blast furnace from iron ore in the presence of carbon at high temperature.
2. _____ Gold in water is "panned" by shaking away dirt and sand.
3. _____ Copper ore in solution is attracted to one electrode in the presence of an electric current.
4. _____ Aluminum metal separates from a solution of aluminum ore dissolved in cryolite at high temperature in the presence of a large electric current.

Name/Date _____

Where Elements Come From 4

Name three metals that are rarely found as free elements.

1. _____

2. _____

3. _____

Name/Date _____

Where Elements Come From 5

What am I? _____

Clue one: There are only a few large deposits of me on Earth, including one near Sudbury, Ontario, in Canada.

Clue two: I am used in the manufacture of coins.

Clue three: Earrings and other jewelry are now made free of me because I can cause skin irritation.

Properties of Matter Warm-ups: Chemical Reactions

Name/Date _____

Chemical Reactions 1

Write "T" for true or "F" for false.

1. _____ All matter is composed of one element or a combination of elements.
2. _____ Elements can break down into many different elements through chemical reactions.
3. _____ When elements combine to form new substances, this is a physical change.
4. _____ As two liquids mix, gas bubbles form and tiny solid crystals appear in the combined liquid. This is evidence of a chemical reaction.

Name/Date _____

Chemical Reactions 2

Circle the words in parentheses that make the sentence true.

1. The materials you have before a chemical reaction are the (reactants / products).
2. After a chemical reaction, you have (the same / different) materials than before the reaction. These are the (reactants / products).

Name/Date _____

Chemical Reactions 3

Write "D" in the blank if the reaction is decomposition, "R" if it replacement, or "S" if it is synthesis.

1. _____ Carbon from charcoal reacts with copper oxide and takes the place of copper, leaving pure copper and carbon dioxide.
2. _____ Magnesium burns in air and combines with oxygen to form magnesium oxide.
3. _____ An electric current breaks water into hydrogen and oxygen gas.

Name/Date _____

Chemical Reactions 4

Name four ways to increase the rate of a chemical reaction.

_____

_____

_____

_____

_____

_____

Name/Date _____

Chemical Reactions 5

Fill in the blanks with words or phrases from the box. One of the choices is used twice.

different than	chemical reactions
reactants	conservation of mass
the same as	products

Even though _____ create _____ that are _____ the _____, their total mass is _____ that of the _____. This is a principle known as the _____.

Properties of Matter Warm-ups: Organizing Elements

Name/Date _____

_____

Organizing Elements 1

Write "T" for true or "F" for false.

1. _____ Mendeleev noticed that the bonding power of elements from lithium to fluorine changed in an orderly way.

2. _____ Mendeleev saw no relation between atomic mass and the properties of elements.

3. _____ Mendeleev left question marks in his chart where he predicted new elements would be found.

Name/Date _____

Organizing Elements 2

Circle the word or number that makes each sentence true.

1. There are about (10 / 100 / 1,000) chemical elements.

2. (All / Some / None) of the elements are very reactive.

3. Reactive elements (rarely / often) form compounds.

Name/Date _____

Organizing Elements 3

Fill in the blanks with the letters of the correct terms.

a. properties   b. atomic mass   c. groups   d. elements

In the 1800s, Dmitri Mendeleev noticed that _____ of _____ had similar _____. He organized them in a chart according to _____.

Name/Date _____

Organizing Elements 4

Circle the words that make each sentence true.

1. The atomic number of an element tells us how many (protons / neutrons / electrons) are (inside / outside) the nucleus.

2. The atoms of a single element always have (the same / a different) number of (neutrons / protons).

Name/Date _____

Organizing Elements 5

Order the following elements by their atomic number from 1 (lowest) to 4 (highest).

1. _____ uranium   2. _____ carbon

3. _____ hydrogen   4. _____ iron

Uranium

Properties of Matter Warm-ups: Organizing Elements (cont.)

Name/Date _____

Organizing Elements 6

Into what three categories are the elements separated?

1. M_____
2. M_____
3. N_____

Name/Date _____

Organizing Elements 7

Write "S" if the pair of elements has similar properties or "NS" if the pair of elements do not have similar properties.

1. ____ potassium and sodium   2. ____ copper and silver

3. ____ iodine and calcium   4. ____ neon and helium

Name/Date _____

Organizing Elements 8

Write "R" if the given pair of elements react at least fairly easily or "NR" if the pair is not reactive.

1. ____ sodium and chlorine   2. ____ helium and neon

3. ____ potassium and calcium   OPEN

4. ____ hydrogen and oxygen

Name/Date _____

Organizing Elements 9

What am I? _____

Clue one: Metals are on my left and nonmetals are on my right.

Clue two: I have columns of families, and every family member has a symbol.

Clue three: I am arranged according to atomic number.

Name/Date _____

_____

Organizing Elements 10

For each state, name two elements that usually exist in that state.

Solid

1. _____

2. _____

Liquid

1. _____

2. _____

Gas

1. _____

2. _____

Properties of Matter Warm-ups: Atoms

Name/Date _____

Atoms 1

Match.

| a. atom | b. compound |
| c. chemical bond | d. molecule |

1. _____ the force that holds separate atoms together

2. _____ a group of joined atoms

3. _____ the smallest particle of an element

4. _____ combined atoms from two or more elements

Name/Date _____

Atoms 2

Unscramble these three types of particles that make up an atom.

1. R O O N P T   _____

2. N O R T U N E   _____

3. C E R N O T E L   _____

Name/Date _____

Atoms 3

What am I? _____

Clue one: I am negatively charged.

Clue two: I move around the nucleus of an atom.

Clue three: A proton has almost 2,000 times more mass than I do.

Name/Date _____

Atoms 4

Label the following parts of an atom with "O" for outside the nucleus or "I" for inside the nucleus.

1. _____ electron

2. _____ neutron

3. _____ proton

Name/Date _____

Atoms 5

Place a check by each sentence that applies to the atomic number.

| 1 H Hydrogen 1.0079 |
| 3 Li Lithium 6.941 | 4 Be Beryllium 9.012 |
| 11 Na Sodium 22.990 | 12 Mg Magnesium 24.305 |

1. _____ It is the number of protons in the nucleus of the atom.

2. _____ It is equal to the atomic mass of an atom.

3. _____ Elements in the Periodic Table are arranged by it.

4. _____ It is found by adding the number of protons in an atom to the number of neutrons.

Properties of Matter Warm-ups: Atoms (cont.)

Name/Date _____

Atoms 6

Draw a line to match the model of the atom developed by each scientist with the closest brief description.

1. Dalton Model
2. Thomson Model
3. Rutherford Model
4. Bohr Model

a. An atom is mostly empty space with electrons orbiting randomly around a tiny core nucleus.

b. An atom is mostly empty space with electrons orbiting in specific shells around a tiny core nucleus.

c. An atom is a tiny solid ball.

d. An atom is a sphere with electrons embedded throughout.

Name/Date _____

Atoms 7

Fill in the blanks.

zero charge protons electrons atom

The total electric _____ on an individual _____ is _____ because normally an atom has an equal number of _____ and _____.

Name/Date _____

Atoms 8

Write "T" for true or "F" for false.

1. _____ Most of the mass of an atom is in the electrons.
2. _____ Positive protons and negative electrons attract each other.
3. _____ The number of neutrons affects atomic mass, but not atomic number.
4. _____ Carbon atoms are common in nature, form many kinds of bonds, and are an important element in living material.

Name/Date _____

Atoms 9

Which electrons in an atom are the only ones involved in bonding? Why is it just these?

_____

_____

_____

_____

Name/Date _____

Atoms 10

Write "C" on the description and example of covalent bonding and "I" on the description and example of ionic bonding.

1. _____ Valence electrons are shared between atoms.
2. _____ Valence electrons move completely from one atom to another.
3. _____ Salt   4. _____ Water

Properties of Matter Warm-ups:
The Periodic Table

Name/Date _____

The Periodic Table 1

Look at your full Periodic Table of the Elements. Below is one cell from the table. Write what type of data is found in the circled position and also write very briefly what that data means.

⑥ C Carbon 12.011	_____
	_____
	_____

Name/Date _____

The Periodic Table 2

Look at your full Periodic Table of the Elements. Below is one cell from the table. Write what type of data is found in the circled position and also write very briefly what that data means.

6 Ⓒ Carbon 12.011	_____
	_____
	_____

Name/Date _____

The Periodic Table 3

Look at your full Periodic Table of the Elements. Below is one cell from the table. Write what type of data is found in the circled position and also write very briefly what that data means.

6 C (Carbon) 12.011	_____
	_____
	_____

Name/Date _____

The Periodic Table 4

Look at your full Periodic Table of the Elements. Below is one cell from the table. Write what type of data is found in the circled position and also write very briefly what that data means.

6 C Carbon (12.011)	_____
	_____
	_____

Name/Date _____

The Periodic Table 5

Write three more properties of elements that could be added to an expanded Periodic Table.

_____

_____

_____

Properties of Matter Warm-ups:
The Periodic Table (cont.)

Name/Date _____

The Periodic Table 6

Look at the cell from the Periodic Table below and write the answers to the questions.

1. _____ What is the chemical symbol for tin?

2. _____ What is the mass of a tin atom in atomic mass units?

3. _____ How many protons are in the nucleus of an atom of tin?

| 50 |
| Sn |
| Tin |
| 118.71 |

Name/Date _____

The Periodic Table 7

Look at the Periodic Table and write the chemical symbol for the element with each property.

1. _____ lightest element
2. _____ heaviest element in nature
3. _____ lightest element with only an approximate atomic mass
4. _____ heaviest artificial element with a permanent name

Name/Date _____

The Periodic Table 8

What am I? _____

Clue one: I am an element and a metal.

Clue two: I am in the fourth period of the Periodic Table.

Clue three: I am the most important material used to make steel.

Name/Date _____

The Periodic Table 9

How many neutrons are most often found in the nucleus of an atom of each element as it occurs in nature?

1. _____ H
2. _____ He
3. _____ K
4. _____ C

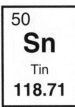

Name/Date _____

The Periodic Table 10

Match each element with its important use.

1. ___ H   a. gas that supports animal life
2. ___ Na   b. gas that glows red-orange in electric signs
3. ___ Ne   c. metal that when combined with chlorine is table salt
4. ___ O   d. gas that when combined with oxygen forms water

Properties of Matter Warm-ups: The Periodic Table (cont.)

Use this page for Warm-ups 11–15 on The Periodic Table on page 29.

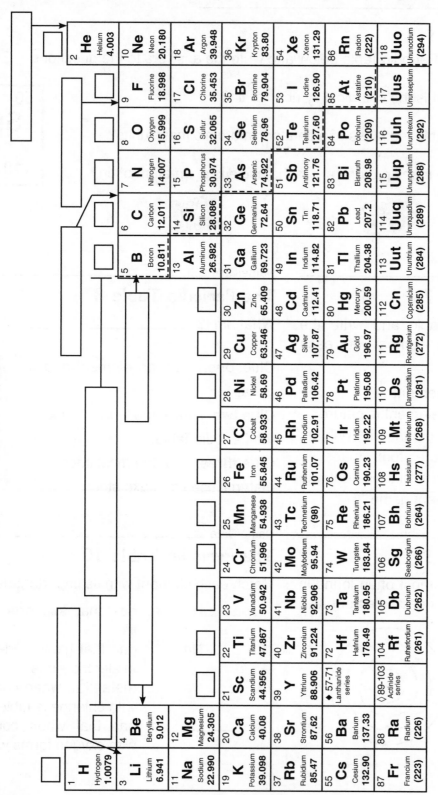

Properties of Matter Warm-ups:
The Periodic Table (cont.)

Name/Date _____

The Periodic Table 11

On the Periodic Table from page 28, fill in the boxes above each column with the 18 Group numbers.

| 5 B Boron 10.811 | 6 C Carbon 12.011 | 7 N Nitrogen 14.007 |
| 13 Al Aluminum 26.982 | 14 Si Silicon 28.086 | 15 P Phosphorus 30.974 |

Name/Date _____

The Periodic Table 12

On the Periodic Table from page 28, fill in the empty boxes with the correct name of each region listed below.

halogens   transition metals

alkaline earth metals   nonmetals

noble gases   metalloids

rare earth elements   alkali metals

Name/Date _____

The Periodic Table 13

On the Periodic Table from page 28, write the number of the property below inside the box of the corresponding group of elements. (Properties may be used more than once.)

1. React with halogens to form salts
2. Least reactive   3. Semiconductors
4. Best conductors of electricity
5. Uncommon, specialized uses
6. Solids, dull, brittle, low density
7. Most reactive and toxic

Name/Date _____

The Periodic Table 14

Explain what a "period" is on the Periodic Table.

_____

_____

_____

_____

_____

_____

Name/Date _____

The Periodic Table 15

Write the group number or numbers for the element family or families that contain elements having the given property.

_____ halogens

_____ very best conductors

_____ least reactive

_____ alkaline earth metals

_____ are atmospheric gases

_____ where rare earths fit

_____ important semiconductors

_____ form strong acids with hydrogen

Properties of Matter Warm-ups: Metals

Name/Date _____

Metals 1

Imagine you are holding a piece of metal such as gold, silver, or iron. List three words you would use to describe it.

1. _____

2. _____

3. _____

Name/Date _____

Metals 2

Unscramble the following properties chemists use to classify an element as a metal.

1. S H S I E N I N S   _____

2. L A B E L Y T I M L I A   _____

3. Y T I T C I L U D   _____

4. E N S H A R D S   _____

Name/Date _____

Metals 3

List three things you encounter on a regular basis that are made possible by the use of metals.

1. _____

2. _____

3. _____

Name/Date _____

Metals 4

For the metals below, write "VR" for very reactive or "LR" for less reactive.

1. _____ Chromium   2. _____ Sodium

3. _____ Gold   4. _____ Iron

Name/Date _____

_____

Metals 5

Match the items below to their group or family on the Periodic Table.

a. Alkali metals

b. Metals in mixed groups

c. Transition metals

d. Alkaline earth metals

1. _____ Group 1

2. _____ Group 2

3. _____ Groups 3 through 12

4. _____ Groups 13 through 16

Cesium

Lead

Platinum

Barium

Properties of Matter Warm-ups: Metals (cont.)

Name/Date _____

Metals 6

An old car in a junk yard is left exposed to water and oxygen. Explain how you think the appearance of the old car will change over time? The chemical reaction of which elements causes this?

_____
_____
_____
_____

Name/Date _____

Metals 7

Fill in the blanks with words from the list.

mixture   alloy   pure   melted

When gold is sold as jewelry, it is rarely _____ gold. Instead, it is a(n) _____ of metals formed by combining _____ gold with other metals such as silver and copper. A gold _____ is strong and durable.

Name/Date _____

Metals 8

Circle the word that makes each sentence true.

1. If a metal easily transmits heat and electricity, it is considered to be a good

    (alloy / conductor).

2. In a malleable metal, the bonds (do / do not) break easily.

3. Thin wire can be made from (malleable / ductile) metals.

4. Metal can sometimes be extracted from (alloys / ores).

Name/Date _____

Metals 9

List four properties that most metals have in common.

1. _____

2. _____

3. _____

4. _____

Name/Date _____

Metals 10

What am I? _____

Clue one: I am made of metal.

Clue two: I have a north and a south pole.

Clue three: I attract objects made of iron or steel.

Properties of Matter Warm-ups: Nonmetals and Metalloids

Name/Date _____

Nonmetals and Metalloids 1

Describe some properties that distinguish metalloids from both metals and nonmetals.

_____

_____

Name/Date _____

Nonmetals and Metalloids 2

Write "T" for true or "F" for false.

1. _____ Most nonmetals are dull.   2. _____ Most nonmetals are malleable.

3. _____ Most metals are denser than most nonmetals.

4. _____ Nonmetals are always good electrical conductors.

Name/Date _____

Nonmetals and Metalloids 3

List three groups or families of nonmetals.

1. _____   2. _____   3. _____

Name/Date _____

Nonmetals and Metalloids 4

Write "N" for nonmetals or "M" for metalloids.

1. _____ silicon   2. _____ carbon

3. _____ hydrogen   4. _____ boron

Name/Date _____

Nonmetals and Metalloids 5

Circle the word in the parentheses that makes each sentence true.

A(n) (valence / external) electron is (closest / farthest) from the nucleus of (an atom / a molecule).

These electrons are involved in (chemical / nuclear) reactions.

Properties of Matter Warm-ups: Nonmetals and Metalloids (cont.)

Name/Date _____

Nonmetals and Metalloids 6

What am I? _____

Clue one: When I'm alone, I am a gas at room temperature.

Clue two: I am very reactive, so I can combine with almost every other element.

Clue three: I am the most abundant element in Earth's crust.

Name/Date _____

Nonmetals and Metalloids 7

Write a good definition of a semiconductor.

_____

_____

_____

_____

_____

_____

Name/Date _____

Nonmetals and Metalloids 8

Place a check next to each of the following that is a good example of an item made with metalloids.

1. _____ computer chips

2. _____ lasers

3. _____ filaments

4. _____ transistors

Name/Date _____

Nonmetals and Metalloids 9

Place a check by each variable that helps determine how well a metalloid can conduct electricity.

1. _____ temperature

2. _____ mass

3. _____ illumination

4. _____ amount of impurities

Name/Date _____

Nonmetals and Metalloids 10

Although steel is a metal and granite is a nonmetal, both share the physical property of hardness. Stainless steel, a steel alloy, and granite are popular choices for kitchen countertops. When it comes to automobile engines, however, steel is used but granite is not. Why?

_____

_____

_____

Properties of Matter Warm-ups:
Halogens and Noble Gases

Name/Date _____

Halogens and Noble Gases 1

The most active nonmetals are called halogens. They are found in Family 17 of the Periodic Table.

List the halogens.

_____

_____

_____

Name/Date _____

Halogens and Noble Gases 2

What am I? _____

1. I am deep red and toxic.

2. I am an element that is liquid at room temperature.

3. I am a halogen.

Name/Date _____

Halogens and Noble Gases 3

Match the noble gas to its use.

| a. helium | b. neon | c. argon |
| d. krypton | e. xenon | f. radon |

1. _____ Used in halogen lightbulbs mixed with iodine and bromine

2. _____ Used in radiotherapy to treat cancer patients

3. _____ Used as an anesthetic

4. _____ Used in blimps and balloons

5. _____ Used in lighted signs to produce a bright red color

6. _____ Used to inflate a scuba diver's dry suit

Name/Date _____

Halogens and Noble Gases 4

Noble gases are the least reactive elements because their outer shells of valence electrons are considered to be full. When they do form compounds, with what family of elements do the noble gases usually bond?

_____

Noble Gases

Name/Date _____

Halogens and Noble Gases 5

The halogens combine with active metals to form salts. What is the salt sodium fluoride used for?

_____

_____

Properties of Matter Warm-ups:
Carbon Compounds

Name/Date _____

Carbon Compounds 1

Why is a compound that contains carbon often called an "organic compound?"

_____
_____
_____
_____
_____

Name/Date _____

Carbon Compounds 2

Write "T" for true or "F" for false.

1. ____ Carbon forms bonds with itself and other elements in many different ways.
2. ____ Carbon is atomic number 6 and has 4 valence electrons available for bonding.
3. ____ Carbon atoms only bond in straight chains.
4. ____ Diamonds, graphite, and fullerene are all forms of carbon.

Name/Date _____

Carbon Compounds 3

Fill in the blanks with words from the list.

properties   liquid   aromatic   boiling   carbon   melting   odors   gaseous

_____ compounds tend to have similar _____. Most have

low _____ points and low _____ points so they are often

_____ or _____ at room temperature. Many organic liquids are

_____, meaning they have strong, distinct _____.

Name/Date _____

Carbon Compounds 4

Put a check in the blank if the material contains one or more carbon compounds.

____ carbon dioxide   ____ salt
____ pure water   ____ protein
____ natural gas   ____ gold
____ plastic   ____ banana

Name/Date _____

Carbon Compounds 5

What am I? _____

Clue one: I am formed of chains of carbon and hydrogen atoms.

Clue two: I burn when I react with oxygen.

Clue three: Liquid forms of me usually mix poorly with water.

Properties of Matter Warm-ups:
Carbon Compounds (cont.)

Name/Date _____

Carbon Compounds 6

Write "N" if the carbon-based substance is a nutrient, or write "P" if it is a poison.

_____ starch   _____ methanol   _____ protein

_____ benzene   _____ glucose   _____ PCBs

_____ fat   _____ naphtha

Name/Date _____

_____

Carbon Compounds 10

Name each compound and write its chemical formula.

H
|
H — C — H
|
H

Name:

_____

Chemical Formula:

_____

Name/Date _____

Carbon Compounds 7

Circle the word or words that best complete the statement.

1. Sugars are the (simplest / most complex) carbohydrates.
2. Many plant stems and roots are rich in (cellulose / protein).
3. Proteins are formed from (lipids / amino acids).

Name/Date _____

Carbon Compounds 8

Draw a line to match the type of substituted hydrocarbon compound on the left to the fact about it on the right.

1. Freon   Gives fragrances to fruits
2. Alcohol   Found in vinegar
3. Acetic acid   Banned chlorofluorocarbon refrigerant
4. Ester   Formed in fermentation of plant material

H   H
| |
H — C — C — H
| |
H   H

Name:

_____

Chemical Formula:

_____

Name/Date _____

Carbon Compounds 9

Name this compound and write its chemical formula. Why is it called an "unsaturated" hydrocarbon?

H   H
| |
H — C = C — H

Name: _____ Chemical Formula: _____

_____

Properties of Matter Warm-ups: Radioactivity

Name/Date _____

Radioactivity 1

Write "yes" or "no" in the boxes to answer the questions about what happens as a result of each type of reaction.

	Reaction Type	
	Chemical	**Nuclear**
1. Does the nucleus of an atom change?		
2. Are new elements created?		
3. Are new substances created?		
4. Can gamma rays be emitted?		

Name/Date _____

Radioactivity 2

Fill in the blanks with words from the list.

alpha   radioactive   half-life   beta

If atoms in a sample of matter are unstable, they undergo _____ decay. They may emit _____ or _____ particles and change into other kinds of atoms. The average amount of time required for half of the original unstable atoms to decay is called the _____.

Name/Date _____

Radioactivity 3

Match the type of radiation with the description.

1. ____ alpha particle
2. ____ beta particle
3. ____ gamma ray
4. ____ neutron

a. uncharged nuclear particle
b. high-energy electro-magnetic emission
c. two protons and two neutrons
d. energetic electron or positron

Name/Date _____

Radioactivity 4

Put in order from 1 (highest) to 3 (lowest) the ability of each type of radiation to penetrate barriers.

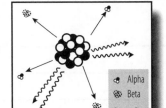

Alpha
Beta
Gamma Rays

_____ alpha particle
_____ beta particle
_____ gamma ray

Name/Date _____

Radioactivity 5

Isotopes are atoms of a single element that vary in the number of neutrons. When isotopes are written as follows, the top number is the total of neutrons and protons, and the bottom number is the atomic number of that element. On your own paper, name the element and write the number of neutrons for each of its isotopes.

1. a. $^{14}_{6}$C   b. $^{12}_{6}$C   2. a. $^{40}_{19}$K   b. $^{39}_{19}$K

3. a. $^{137}_{55}$Cs   b. $^{133}_{55}$Cs

Properties of Matter Warm-ups: Rare Earth and Heavy Elements

Name/Date _____

Rare Earth and Heavy Elements 1

What are we? _____

Clue one: We are the group that comes between the alkaline earth metals and the transition metals.

Clue two: We are placed below the Periodic Table for convenience.

Clue three: We are metals that are soft, shiny, and malleable.

Name/Date _____

Rare Earth and Heavy Elements 2

Circle the rare earth elements in the list below.

gold   promethium   tungsten

krypton   plutonium   gadolinium

dysprosium   uranium

Name/Date _____

Rare Earth and Heavy Elements 3

Write "T" for true or "F" for false.

1. _____ There are only three rare elements.
2. _____ Processes exist today that make it easier to purify the rare earth elements from their oxides.
3. _____ Some artificial elements can only be created a few atoms at a time under laboratory conditions and survive only a fraction of a second.
4. _____ In the Periodic Table, all the elements after uranium are created only in laboratories or nuclear reactors.

Name/Date _____

Rare Earth and Heavy Elements 4

Circle the words in parentheses to make the paragraph true.

Heavy elements above atomic number 84 are all (stable / radioactive). The (nuclei / electrons) of these elements change into those of others. Uranium is the heaviest (natural / artificial) element. Uranium is (stable / radioactive), so it begins a chain of decay that leads to elements like radon and radium. The chain ends with (stable / radioactive) lead.

Name/Date _____

Rare Earth and Heavy Elements 5

Where do artificial elements "fit" in the Periodic Table? What range of atomic numbers represent the artificial elements?

_____

_____

_____

Properties of Matter Warm-ups:
The Periodic Table of the Elements

Nonmetals

Metals

Transition Metals

1 **H** Hydrogen 1.0079			
Atomic Number → 1 **H** ← Atomic Symbol			
Element Name → Hydrogen 1.0079 ← Atomic Mass (most stable isotope of radioactive elements in parentheses)			

																	2 **He** Helium 4.003
1 **H** Hydrogen 1.0079																	
3 **Li** Lithium 6.941	4 **Be** Beryllium 9.012											5 **B** Boron 10.811	6 **C** Carbon 12.011	7 **N** Nitrogen 14.007	8 **O** Oxygen 15.999	9 **F** Fluorine 18.998	10 **Ne** Neon 20.180
11 **Na** Sodium 22.990	12 **Mg** Magnesium 24.305											13 **Al** Aluminum 26.982	14 **Si** Silicon 28.086	15 **P** Phosphorus 30.974	16 **S** Sulfur 32.065	17 **Cl** Chlorine 35.453	18 **Ar** Argon 39.948
19 **K** Potassium 39.098	20 **Ca** Calcium 40.08	21 **Sc** Scandium 44.956	22 **Ti** Titanium 47.867	23 **V** Vanadium 50.942	24 **Cr** Chromium 51.996	25 **Mn** Manganese 54.938	26 **Fe** Iron 55.845	27 **Co** Cobalt 58.933	28 **Ni** Nickel 58.69	29 **Cu** Copper 63.546	30 **Zn** Zinc 65.409	31 **Ga** Gallium 69.723	32 **Ge** Germanium 72.64	33 **As** Arsenic 74.922	34 **Se** Selenium 78.96	35 **Br** Bromine 79.904	36 **Kr** Krypton 83.80
37 **Rb** Rubidium 85.47	38 **Sr** Strontium 87.62	39 **Y** Yttrium 88.906	40 **Zr** Zirconium 91.224	41 **Nb** Niobium 92.906	42 **Mo** Molybdenum 95.94	43 **Tc** Technetium (98)	44 **Ru** Ruthenium 101.07	45 **Rh** Rhodium 102.91	46 **Pd** Palladium 106.42	47 **Ag** Silver 107.87	48 **Cd** Cadmium 112.41	49 **In** Indium 114.82	50 **Sn** Tin 118.71	51 **Sb** Antimony 121.76	52 **Te** Tellurium 127.60	53 **I** Iodine 126.90	54 **Xe** Xenon 131.29
55 **Cs** Cesium 132.90	56 **Ba** Barium 137.33	◆ 57-71 Lanthanide series (rare earth elements)	72 **Hf** Hafnium 178.49	73 **Ta** Tantalum 180.95	74 **W** Tungsten 183.84	75 **Re** Rhenium 186.21	76 **Os** Osmium 190.23	77 **Ir** Iridium 192.22	78 **Pt** Platinum 195.08	79 **Au** Gold 196.97	80 **Hg** Mercury 200.59	81 **Tl** Thallium 204.38	82 **Pb** Lead 207.2	83 **Bi** Bismuth 208.98	84 **Po** Polonium (209)	85 **At** Astatine (210)	86 **Rn** Radon (222)
87 **Fr** Francium (223)	88 **Ra** Radium (226)	◇ 89-103 Actinide series (radioactive earth elements)	104 **Rf** Rutherfordium (261)	105 **Db** Dubnium (262)	106 **Sg** Seaborgium (266)	107 **Bh** Bohrium (264)	108 **Hs** Hassium (277)	109 **Mt** Meitnerium (268)	110 **Ds** Darmstadtium (281)	111 **Rg** Roentgenium (272)	112 **Cn** Copernicium (285)	113 **Uut** Ununtrium (284)	114 **Uuq** Ununquadium (289)	115 **Uup** Ununpentium (288)	116 **Uuh** Ununhexium (292)	117 **Uus** Ununseptium (294)	118 **Uuo** Ununoctium (294)

◆	57 **La** Lanthanum 138.91	58 **Ce** Cerium 140.12	59 **Pr** Praseodymium 140.91	60 **Nd** Neodymium 144.24	61 **Pm** Promethium (145)	62 **Sm** Samarium 150.36	63 **Eu** Europium 151.96	64 **Gd** Gadolinium 157.25	65 **Tb** Terbium 158.92	66 **Dy** Dysprosium 162.50	67 **Ho** Holmium 164.93	68 **Er** Erbium 167.26	69 **Tm** Thulium 168.93	70 **Yb** Ytterbium 173.04	71 **Lu** Lutetium 174.97
◇	89 **Ac** Actinium (227)	90 **Th** Thorium 232.04	91 **Pa** Protactinium 231.04	92 **U** Uranium 238.03	93 **Np** Neptunium (237)	94 **Pu** Plutonium (244)	95 **Am** Americium (243)	96 **Cm** Curium (247)	97 **Bk** Berkelium (247)	98 **Cf** Californium (251)	99 **Es** Einsteinium (252)	100 **Fm** Fermium (257)	101 **Md** Mendelevium (258)	102 **No** Nobelium (259)	103 **Lr** Lawrencium (262)

Answer Keys

Forms of Matter 1 (page 2)
Answers may vary. Possible answers given.
1. smooth or cool
2. sights like water and feelings like wetness
3. smells like perfume and powder
4. feelings like coldness and shivering and smells like chlorine

Forms of Matter 2 (page 2)
1. Air   2. air   3. Water   4. Water

Forms of Matter 3 (page 2)
d, a, e, b, c

Forms of Matter 4 (page 2)
1. Variable, but things like ice and bricks
2. Variable, but things like water and gasoline
3. Variable, but things like steam and air

Forms of Matter 5 (page 2)
two different rocks: smoothness, hardness, shape
water and air: temperature
two different pieces of metal: smoothness, hardness, shape, flammability
steam and natural gas: temperature, flammability

Forms of Matter 6 (page 3)
1. Variable, but matter such as blueberries and jeans
2. Variable, but matter such as grass and broccoli
3. Variable, but matter such as snow and paper
4. Variable, but matter such as dirt and wood

Forms of Matter 7 (page 3)
1. ODOR   2. TEXTURE   3. SIZE
4. TASTE or STATE   5. COLOR

Forms of Matter 8 (page 3)
Variable, but an item like an apple with properties such as firm and shiny and without properties like soft and discolored

Forms of Matter 9 (page 3)
Variable, but things such as cotton and denim; rice and cheese; oil and gasoline; steel and iron

Forms of Matter 10 (page 3)
Cooking gas, sawdust, spoiled food, and paint should be checked.

What Is a "Property"? 1 (page 4)
1. temperature, boiling point
2. temperature, freezing point
3. state

What Is a "Property"? 2 (page 4)
Variable, including descriptions such as color, weight, temperature, firmness, and smoothness

What Is a "Property"? 3 (page 4)
Variable, including descriptions such as weight, size, temperature, state, and color

What Is a "Property"? 4 (page 4)
Variable, but should include that the difference is that characteristic properties are the properties that make any given matter unique.

What Is a "Property"? 5 (page 4)
a. 3   b. 1   c. 2   d. 4

What Is a "Property"? 6 (page 5)
A rock

What Is a "Property"? 7 (page 5)
1. P   2. M   3. P   4. M   5. P   6. M

What Is a "Property"? 8 (page 5)
characteristic, vary, melting point, water

What Is a "Property"? 9 (page 5)
mixture, matter, solution, salt, dissolved, water

What Is a "Property"? 10 (page 5)
A chemical change can break down a compound into elements.

Measuring Matter 1 (page 6)
Variable, but answer should indicate that mass is a property of matter that can be measured. It is the amount of matter in an object.

Measuring Matter 2 (page 6)
1. No   2. Yes   3. Yes   4. No

Measuring Matter 3 (page 6)
A kilogram

Measuring Matter 4 (page 6)
Change regularly to irregularly, slope to level, fall to rise, container to water, water to object.

Measuring Matter 5 (page 6)
1. b   2. c   3. a   4. d

Measuring Matter 6 (page 7)
1. kilogram   2. milliliter   3. centimeter
4. liter   5. cubic meter 6. gram

Measuring Matter 7 (page 7)
Sentences #1, #4, and #5 should be circled.

Measuring Matter 8 (page 7)
1. 68   2. 86   3. 104   4. 41
5. -4   6. -40

Measuring Matter 9 (page 7)
1. balance, mass   2. metric system

Measuring Matter 10 (page 7)
1. 1; 0.01; 1   2. 1; 0.01; 1

Density 1 (page 8)
1. F   2. F   3. T   4. T

Density 2 (page 8)
1. A softball is filled with solid material while the middle of a basketball is all air. The solid material inside the softball is much denser than air.
2. 0.4 g/cm³

Density 3 (page 8)
1. Can of diet soda should be circled; reason should include that the sugar solution in regular soda is denser.
2. Kernel of popped popcorn should be circled; reason should include that popped popcorn is less dense.

Density 4 (page 8)
1. Answer should include that helium is less dense than air.
2. Answer should include that the air inside the balloon is the same density as the air outside the balloon, so the weight of the balloon material causes it to sink.

Density 5 (page 8)
property, mass, volume, float, sink

Density 6 (page 9)
1. liquid   2. on the surface
3. Variable, but should indicate that ice is less dense than water and therefore floats on the surface of a lake.

Density 7 (page 9)
mass and density, temperature and pressure

Density 8 (page 9)
oil

Density 9 (page 9)
1. No   2. Yes   3. No   4. No

Density 10 (page 9)
Variable, but may include ice and ice cream

Particle Ideas 1 (page 10)
Possible answers: Collection of identical particles: a bag of rice; Collection of varying particles: a bag of bird seed containing different kinds of seed

Particle Ideas 2 (page 10)
1. A piece of glass should be circled; explanation may include that it is easier to break glass than metal.
2. A bag of rice should be circled; explanation may include that it is easier to separate grains from each other than to break apart one grain.

Particle Ideas 3 (page 10)
a. 2   b. 3   c. 1   d. 4

Particle Ideas 4 (page 10)
1. L   2. T   3. L   4. T

Particle Ideas 5 (page 10)
particles, Smoke, mixture, colloid

Particle Ideas 6 (page 11)
1. F   2. T   3. F

Particle Ideas 7 (page 11)
Dalton proposed the atomic theory of matter. His model was of the atom and showed that atoms were tiny particles that shared characteristic properties.

Particle Ideas 8 (page 11)
1. d, a   2. b, c

Particle Ideas 9 (page 11)
Variable, but should include that when atoms bond, they give, receive, or share electrons in order to form a compound.

Particle Ideas 10 (page 11)
In any order:
1. neutron   2. electron   3. proton

Properties of Solids 1 (page 12)
1. T   2. T   3. F   4. F

Properties of Solids 2 (page 12)
Variable, but may include that solids keep their shape unless broken and cannot flow and that liquids take the shapes of their containers and can flow.

Properties of Solids 3 (page 12)
Change loosely to tightly, random to fixed, and formless to definite.

Properties of Solids 4 (page 12)
In any order: definite shape, definite mass, and definite volume

Properties of Solids 5 (page 12)
1. C   2. A   3. A   4. C

Properties of Liquids 1 (page 13)
1. c   2. a   3. b   4. d

Properties of Liquids 2 (page 13)
Variable, but should include that the particles that make up liquids are able to move or slide past each other

Properties of Liquids 3 (page 13)
1. F   2. T   3. T   4. T

Properties of Liquids 4 (page 13)
1. faster   2. cool   3. temperature
4. compress

Properties of Liquids 5 (page 13)
Variable, but answer should indicate that the maple syrup will fall slower than the water. Answer should indicate that maple syrup has a higher viscosity or that water has a lower viscosity.

Properties of Gases 1 (page 14)
water vapor

Properties of Gases 2 (page 14)
Variable, but may include the following:
1. Gases generally cannot be seen.
2. Gases expand to fill their containers.
3. Gases can be compressed.

Properties of Gases 3 (page 14)
volume, container, pressure, compress

Properties of Gases 4 (page 14)
Variable, but should include that the cooler temperature would cause the pressure to drop.

Properties of Gases 5 (page 14)
1. OXYGEN   2. STEAM
3. HELIUM   4. NITROGEN

Physical and Chemical Changes 1 (page 15)
1. new   2. precipitate
3. physical   4. always

Physical and Chemical Changes 2 (page 15)
physical, chemical

Physical and Chemical Changes 3 (page 15)
Variable, but may include seeing the wood turn to ashes, smelling the smoke, feeling heat from the fireplace, or hear the crackling of the fire.

Physical and Chemical Changes 4 (page 15)
The following should be circled:
1. crumpling a piece of paper
2. painting an iron gate
3. molding clay
4. heating pasta sauce

Physical and Chemical Changes 5 (page 15)
1. F   2. T   3. F   4. T

Physical and Chemical Changes 6 (page 16)
Variable, but may include that energy is released, a gas is produced, a solid is formed, a permanent color change occurs, a new odor is produced, or the change that occurred is irreversible.

Physical and Chemical Changes 7 (page 16)
No; if the water evaporates, the salt will be left behind.

Physical and Chemical Changes 8 (page 16)
1. F   2. T   3. F

Physical and Chemical Changes 9 (page 16)
chemical bond, Reactive, unreactive

Physical and Chemical Changes 10 (page 16)
1. No; the heat from the oven broke down the chemical bonds of the ingredients in the cookies so that they are no longer easily separated from each other.
2. Variable, but answers may include that the baking powder reacted with the other ingredients to cause the cookies to rise or that the cookies browned as a result of the sugar reacting to the heat.

Changes of State 1 (page 17)
1. solid, fixed   2. rearrange, do
3. energy   4. faster, rises

Changes of State 2 (page 17)
1. F   2. T   3. T   4. T

Changes of State 3 (page 17)
Variable, but a good answer would be that energy is used to change structure from solid to liquid or liquid to gas. Energy does not go toward changing temperature during melting or boiling.

Changes of State 4 (page 17)
1. Variable, but vaporization example may include water evaporating into air at room temperature
2. Variable, but sublimation example may include water turning into steam when it reaches its boiling point

Changes of State 5 (page 17)
Items #1, #3, and #4 should be checked.

Elements and Compounds 1 (page 18)
particles, elements, (any order: solids, liquids, gases)

Elements and Compounds 2 (page 18)
Items #1 and #2 should be checked.

Elements and Compounds 3 (page 18)
1. c   2. a   3. d   4. b

Elements and Compounds 4 (page 18)
Elements are made from one kind of atom while compounds are made from more than one kind of atom.

Elements and Compounds 5 (page 18)
carbon dioxide

Elements and Compounds 6 (page 19)
1. T   2. T   3. F   4. T

Elements and Compounds 7 (page 19)
1. C   2. C   3. E   4. E

Elements and Compounds 8 (page 19)
Statements #1, #2, and #3 should be checked.

Elements and Compounds 9 (page 19)
1. a   2. b   3. c   4. d

Elements and Compounds 10 (page 19)
compound, elements, properties

Where Elements Come From 1 (page 20)
No, many elements are not stable in their pure form, so they combine with other elements.

Where Elements Come From 2 (page 20)
1. T   2. T   3. F   4. T

Where Elements Come From 3 (page 20)
1. C   2. Ph   3. E   4. E

Where Elements Come From 4 (page 20)
Variable, but may include iron, aluminum, sodium, or potassium.

Where Elements Come From 5 (page 20)
nickel

Chemical Reactions 1 (page 21)
1. T   2. F   3. F   4. T

Chemical Reactions 2 (page 21)
1. reactants   2. different, products

Chemical Reactions 3 (page 21)
1. R   2. S   3. D

Chemical Reactions 4 (page 21)
Variable, but may include increasing temperature, adding a catalyst, changing the medium in which the reaction occurs, or using a higher concentration of reactants.

Chemical Reactions 5 (page 21)
chemical reactions, products, different than, reactants, the same as, reactants, conservation of mass

Organizing Elements 1 (page 22)
1. T   2. F   3. T

Organizing Elements 2 (page 22)
1. 100   2. Some   3. often

Organizing Elements 3 (page 22)
c, d, a, b

Organizing Elements 4 (page 22)
1. protons, inside   2. the same, protons

Organizing Elements 5 (page 22)
1. 4   2. 2   3. 1   4. 3

Organizing Elements 6 (page 23)
1. Metals   2. Metalloids   3. Nonmetals

Organizing Elements 7 (page 23)
1. S   2. S   3. NS   4. S

Organizing Elements 8 (page 23)
1. R   2. NR   3. R   4. R

Organizing Elements 9 (page 23)
The Periodic Table

Organizing Elements 10 (page 23)
Variable, but answers may include solids such as sodium, iron, or nickel; liquids such as mercury and bromine; and gases such as oxygen, helium, or neon

Atoms 1 (page 24)
1. c   2. d   3. a   4. b

Atoms 2 (page 24)
1. PROTON   2. NEUTRON   3. ELECTRON

Atoms 3 (page 24)
An electron

Atoms 4 (page 24)
1. O   2. I   3. I

Atoms 5 (page 24)
Sentences #1 and #3 should be checked.

Atoms 6 (page 25)
1. c   2. d   3. a   4. b

Atoms 7 (page 25)
charge, atom, zero, protons, electrons

Atoms 8 (page 25)
1. F   2. T   3. T   4. T

Atoms 9 (page 25)
The valence, or outermost, electrons are the ones involved in bonding because atoms like to have full valence shells.

Atoms 10 (page 25)
1. C   2. I   3. I   4. C

The Periodic Table 1–4 (page 26)
1. Atomic number, number of protons in the nucleus of each atom
2. Chemical symbol, accepted abbreviation for element
3. Name of element, accepted name identifying the element
4. Atomic mass, mass of the nucleus of an atom of the element in atomic mass units

The Periodic Table 5 (page 26)
Variable, but possibilities include density, melting point, boiling point, state at room temperature, hardness (if solid), electron configuration, and so on.

The Periodic Table 6 (page 27)
1. Sn   2. 118.71 amu   3. 50

The Periodic Table 7 (page 27)
1. H   2. U
3. Tc (Note: This element is the one with the lowest atomic number while having its atomic mass given in parentheses.)
4. Cn

The Periodic Table 8 (page 27)
iron

The Periodic Table 9 (page 27)
1. 0   2. 2   3. 20   4. 6

The Periodic Table 10 (page 27)
1. d   2. c   3. b   4. a

The Periodic Table 11–13 (pages 28–29)
See Periodic Table answers on page 46.

The Periodic Table 14 (page 29)
A period is one row of the Periodic Table. Properties of elements vary across a period.

The Periodic Table 15 (page 29)
17   halogens
11   very best conductors
18   least reactive
2   alkaline earth metals

15, 16, 18   are atmospheric gases
3   where rare earths fit
14   important semiconductors
17   form strong acids with hydrogen

Metals 1 (page 30)
Variable, depending upon the metal and its form, but possibilities are: shiny, cool, hard, silvery, gray, reflective, dense, sharp, and so on. (Students should be allowed a wide latitude here.)

Metals 2 (page 30)
1. SHININESS   2. MALLEABILITY
3. DUCTILITY   4. HARDNESS

Metals 3 (page 30)
Variable, possibilities include silverware, shelving, many parts of vehicles, appliances, cabinets, hardware, doorknobs, many kinds of building materials, wires, and so on.

Metals 4 (page 30)
1. LR   2. VR   3. LR   4. LR

Metals 5 (page 30)
1. a   2. d   3. c   4. b

Metals 6 (page 31)
The car will rust and decay. Rusting areas will have a reddish-brown appearance. This happens when iron and oxygen react in the presence of water.

Metals 7 (page 31)
pure, mixture, melted, alloy

Metals 8 (page 31)
1. conductor   2. do not   3. ductile   4. ores

Metals 9 (page 31)
Variable, but could include hard, shiny, good conductors, higher melting points, and so on.

Metals 10 (page 31)
a magnet

Nonmetals and Metalloids 1 (page 32)
Some metalloids can behave as "semiconductors," which have higher and more controllable resistance to conduction of electricity than metals. Metalloids have lower melting points than metals and some have characteristics more like nonmetals.

Nonmetals and Metalloids 2 (page 32)
1. T   2. F   3. T   4. F

Nonmetals and Metalloids 3 (page 32)
Group 16, Group 17, Group 18

Nonmetals and Metalloids 4 (page 32)
1. M   2. N   3. N   4. M

Nonmetals and Metalloids 5 (page 32)
valence, farthest, an atom, chemical

Nonmetals and Metalloids 6 (page 33)
oxygen

Nonmetals and Metalloids 7 (page 33)
A semiconductor is a material that conducts electricity, but not quite as well as good conductors like silver or copper. Their ability to conduct can be controlled by adding impurities.

Nonmetals and Metalloids 8 (page 33)
Items #1 and #4 should be checked.

Nonmetals and Metalloids 9 (page 33)
Items #1, #3, and #4 should be checked.

Nonmetals and Metalloids 10 (page 33)
Variable, but a possible answer is that it would be very difficult to make auto parts from granite. Granite is much less flexible than steel, so under stress, thin pieces would break.

Halogens and Noble Gases 1 (Page 34)
fluorine, chlorine, bromine, iodine, astatine

Halogens and Noble Gases 2 (Page 34)
bromine

Halogens and Noble Gases 3 (Page 34)
1. d   2. f   3. e   4. a   5. b   6. c

Halogens and Noble Gases 4 (Page 34)
halogens

Halogens and Noble Gases 5 (Page 34)
It fluoridates drinking water to discourage the growth of bacteria on teeth.

Carbon Compounds 1 (Page 35)
"Organic" means living matter. Living organisms make carbon compounds, so many, but not all, of these compounds are called organic.

Carbon Compounds 2 (Page 35)
1. T   2. T   3. F   4. T

Carbon Compounds 3 (Page 35)
Carbon, properties, melting, boiling, liquid, gaseous, aromatic, odors

Carbon Compounds 4 (Page 35)
Checked: carbon dioxide, protein, natural gas, plastic, banana

Carbon Compounds 5 (Page 35)
hydrocarbon

Carbon Compounds 6 (Page 36)
N starch   P methanol   N protein
P benzene   N glucose   P PCBs
N fat   P naphtha

Carbon Compounds 7 (Page 36)
1. simplest   2. cellulose   3. amino acids

Carbon Compounds 8 (Page 36)
Freon: Banned chlorofluorocarbon refrigerant
Alcohol: Formed in fermentation of plant material
Acetic acid: Found in vinegar
Ester: Gives fragrances to fruits

Carbon Compounds 9 (Page 36)
ethylene (also known as ethene)

C_2H_4

Because the two carbons use a double bond, there are two fewer than the maximum number of hydrogens

Carbon Compounds 10 (Page 36)
methane   ethane

CH_4 C_2H_6

Radioactivity 1 (Page 37)

	Chemical	Nuclear
1.	no	yes
2.	no	yes
3.	yes	yes
4.	no	yes

Radioactivity 2 (Page 37)
radioactive, alpha/beta, beta/alpha, half-life

Radioactivity 3 (Page 37)
1. c   2. d   3. b   4. a

Radioactivity 4 (Page 37)
3: alpha particle   2: beta particle   1: gamma ray

Radioactivity 5 (Page 37)
1. Carbon   a. 8   b. 6
2. Potassium   a. 21 b. 20
3. Cesium   a. 82 b. 78

Rare Earth and Heavy Elements 1 (Page 38)
Rare earth elements

Rare Earth and Heavy Elements 2 (Page 38)
Promethium, gadolinium, and dysprosium should be circled.

Rare Earth and Heavy Elements 3 (Page 38)
1. F   2. T   3. T   4. T

Rare Earth and Heavy Elements 4 (Page 38)
radioactive, nuclei, natural, radioactive, stable

Rare Earth and Heavy Elements 5 (Page 38)
Artificial elements fit in the last period of the Periodic Table in Groups 3 through 18. They have atomic numbers 93 through 118.

Answers for The Periodic Table 11–13 (pages 28–29)

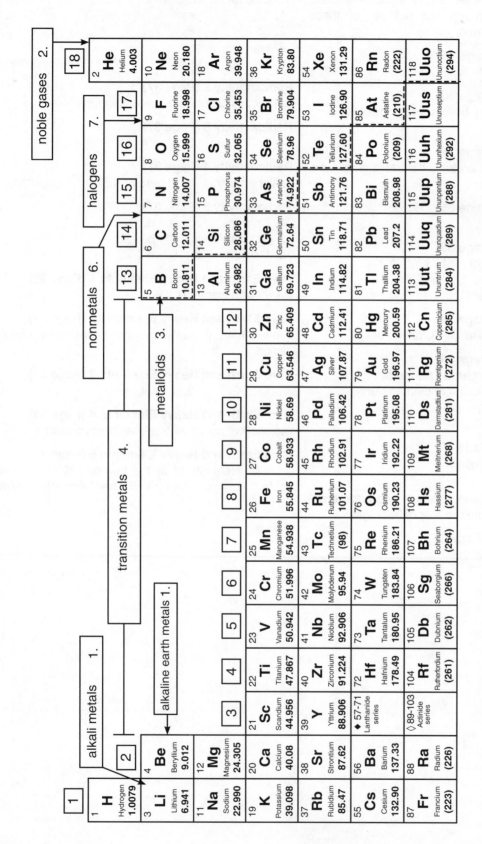